Can I Eat This Candy?

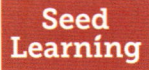

Can I eat
this candy?

Yes, you can.

You can eat
that candy.

Can I borrow
this scooter?

Yes, you can.

You can borrow
that scooter.

Can I have
this backpack?

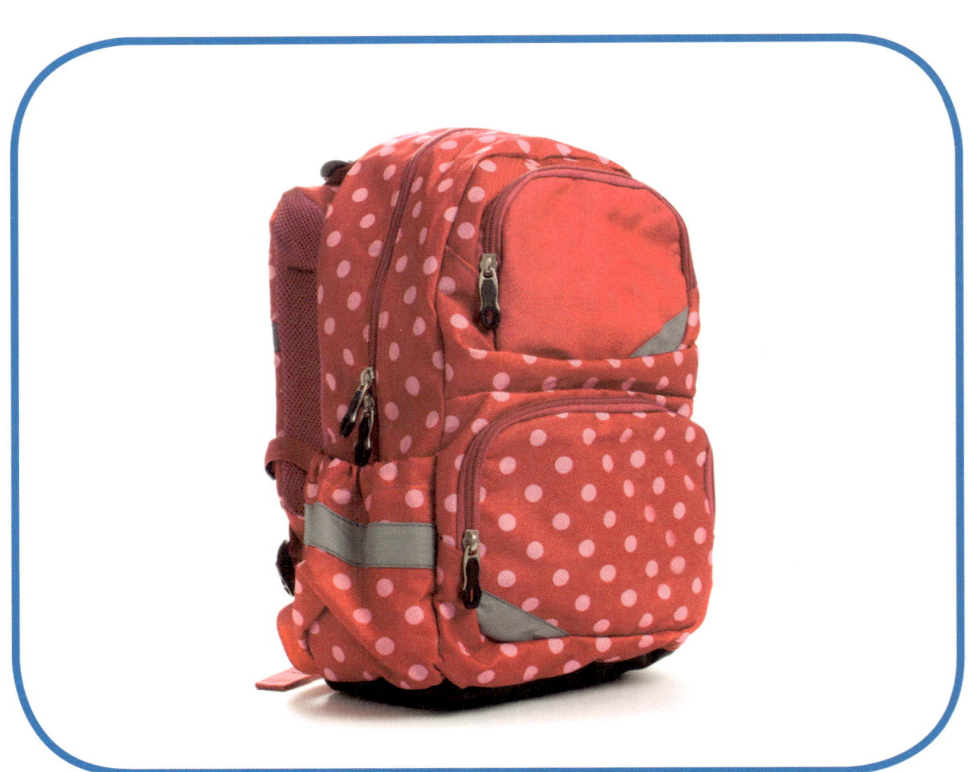

Yes, you can.

You can have
that backpack.

Can I open this door?

Yes, you can.

You can open
that door.

Can I color
this picture?

Yes, you can.

You can color
that picture.

Can I pet
this goat?

Yes, you can.

You can pet
that goat.

Can I touch this pot?

No, you can't!

You can't touch
that pot.

Let's learn about Valentine's Day.

February

Sunday	Monday	Tuesday	Wednesday	Thursday	Friday	Saturday
	1	2	3	4	5	6
7	8	9	10	11	12	13
(14)	15	16	17	18	19	20
21	22	23	24	25	26	27
28						

Trace the word February
and circle the date.